POETRY NOW

1994 POETS

Edited by Veronica Hannon

First published in Great Britain in 1993 by
POETRY NOW
1-2 Wainman Road, Woodston,
Peterborough, PE2 7BU

Contents

Foreword

Poetry Now has kicked off 1994 with a contemporary collection of poetry from across the world. This collection celebrates the wide variety and strength of writing today.

One of the most difficult things about editing this collection was having to limit it to only one hundred and twenty poems. The poetry we received had such a depth of commitment, variety of voice, reason and emotion that it soon became obvious what an important and relevant book it would be both for today and for future generations.

Covering a wide range of styles from free verse to tightly written rhyme, these poets speak with candour, wit, insight and above all honesty; each one demands to be read and re-read. More than anything else what they offer the reader is undeniable proof of the hope and tenacity that poetry - no matter what our current situation - can always provide.

The Edge

Graceful gulls, plain level with my eye
On this high promontory.
Eye to restless eye
I stand, you hover, I fear
You, who understand the elemental power
Of wind, and rain and sea.
White feathered, calm
You look at me
Impersonal, glittering.
Winter sunbright air,
A purification rite on naked skin
Is clean and cold,
Free of earth. I envy you your freedom.
Your wings beat rhythms
In the crystal light
While you fly.

Erica Beynon

Visitors

She boils
the water

looks
at the
empty cup

Already
she can hear
the voices

outside

gathering

Victor Tapner

A Child in Every Heart

There is a child in every heart,
That is somehow left behind,
In a stable or in the bulrushes
Or deliberately lost on some scraggy
hillside.

A dependent child that gazes in wonder,
At moonlight which disturbs the fitful
sleep of so called maturity.

A child kicking to be reborn,
When drudgery steals
that yearning for adventure -
A child clasping your hand
To guide you to wonders of creation.

A child who sees fresh colours,
When all has faded into monochrome
familiarity,
Who finds a miracle
In the riotous melody of dawn.

A child who awakes to seek treasure,
Fight a battle, fall in love,
While the adult shuffles through
misty routines,
familiar headlines of broken promises,
broken dreams, broken homes, broken lives.
The child hears a symphony,
Composed of promises
of dreams fulfilled.

There is a child inside your heart,
Who can build a rainbow out of threads,
You took to be the strands of loss.

John Marrison

In the Andes

I didn't write down what we ate
I only wrote down the wind
And the fig tree with washing
Blown at its roots.

I didn't write down the bus
Or the travelling white men
With rucksacks and tee shirts
Who looked wrong out of place.

I saw only the Indian boys
With the faces of grave men
Tethered to sheep. Smut on their cheeks
And sun in their eyes. Coca cola baseball
Caps and small rubbed away toes.

Kathleen Mary Gibbons

Untitled

Out of a darkness purely physical
I draw the boundaries of my soul:
The birth of music and the birth of Time:
The ecstasy of the mountains;
And the awakening of sacrifice.
These things are the proof of my life.
For I am the harpist of Jehovah,
The first green sheaf of holiness,
The fair-winged bird of Heaven and of Earth.
Behold the voice of the Master
Whose prophecies run in my veins. Behold
The honour of God is near you.
I am he who walks in the first darkness:
Abel - Inheritor of Hell.

John D Ballam

Miner

Once I used dread the dark, the hardness,
how it could catch me watching my own smallness
or listening for fear (my second heartbeat)
always listening for the quiet crack of an opening
or the low rumble of stone.

We believed that we lived on the brink of the terrible
toughened with the strength of overcoming fear
and every month brought gories from South Africa -
of parallel collapse, of poorly slatted shafts,
of glory for our brothers underground.

Then we would go threading women in the town,
travel for hours in the hot jittering dust
to find that women only want a drunkard
or a clown and soon I began to stay behind.

They hate to call me miner as I have no miner's wife
and mothers fear to leave me with their sons
but I go below where I can tell the light
that fades a lady blondly from my eye and where I know
a pure one when she draws me through the deep.

Sometimes I have been down so long
I yearn to sink inside her and be gone.
I know some morning I may be found out.
They will come upon me where I lie
prostrate, naked, my fingers in her mouth.

Siobhán Campbell

Adlestrop Revisited

No. They've forgotten Adlestrop -
No platform now to show the name,
No sign of any station left,
Only the shining rails the same,

And the old stationmaster's house,
And photos in the porch to show
The little platform and the staff
In uniforms of long ago.

It was a day in early June,
Quiet, and not a soul in sight,
A soft and sleepy afternoon -
Just the cowparsley foaming white

And buttercups and dandelions;
And in the willows by the rails
Thrushes and tits and warblers sang -
And later, maybe, nightingales.

A D Melville

Gynt's Onion

'So,' he said, 'I'll understand the simple thing,'
And took an onion, tore off paper coats,
Then some that were part flesh.
Next, thick integuments: white, tumid, cellular;
Green longitudes, he hoped, marked out a map.
But mad, lust-dieted Peer threw them aside;
Wept, with stinging eyes,
Peer, Peter, Peter Piper, pecker-picker,
Foiled like any pop philosopher
Or folio-foundered scholar; the fool anatomist
Who cut open a heart to find out why it beat,
And cut it dead. Let him string out his sorrows,
Weep his onion tears.

Onions make sauce, make soup, make sense -
Smell your fingers, onion-searcher; you breathe in
The peasant-breath, the rich broth, catch the whiff,
Scent, fragrant reek of the real, the globe, the onion.

Kate Wallbank

Approaching Tea-Time

With the lamp behind her melting
Puddles of light into the dusk,
My grandmother, in shadow, raising
And sweeping her stiff arms,
First jerks then billows the cloth,
(old cloth - white, starched linen)
And guides it down onto the table top.
A coal cracks on the fire.
Cups clink on the tray.
We wait.

Now, forty years on,
Afternoon throws down evening,
Onto February's snow. (Old snow,
blue grey and stained yellow by street lamps).
Inside, beside the window,
My mother - grown stiff limbed and white-haired -
Smoothes another cloth upon another table-top.
The television murmurs,
The kettle whistles.
We wait.

The creased day ends.
Shadows fold into shadows.
Everything is different,
Nothing ever changes.

Paula Fitzpatrick

Creation

Words, ideas,
Like summer flies dancing in my heat-hazed mind,
Images, sounds,
Float before me, elusive to my web.
Enforced thoughts
Plague the writer's ready hand, yet
Inspiration comes
To those who wait then trawl a heavy net
Of words.

D Mariana Robinson

Medina Road

A small squat woman she
touches his leather
with her fingertip,
as if to speak,
but cocks her head
instead
at something.

To look at her face
might be to know exactly
how careful to be:
as if
with nothing.

'Back soon,'
she says first.

We watch as she stands
and holds her self
with her fingertip
still
on his jacket.

An arthritic greatcoat she
Jumps the queue
and the man at enquiries,
perhaps, rather sly,
gives a little
worn smile.

Phil May

Look

Look, then turn
Away and learn
That life, so fragile,
Held in mortal cradle,
That rocked by the
Hand of death,
As certain
As each shallow breath,
Can end,
Can stop,
Can cease to be.
A life,
Though led in purity,
Does not extend
To infinity.
You cannot change your destiny.

Neil Mutter

Domine, da mihi aquam

The world of ours is plunged in the brotherly blood,
Intense grief and anger surges in my heart like a flood
When I hear limbless children in their agony scream,
And see their shattered bodies on TV and in my dreams . . .
Just men calling the villains to their senses - is in vain
So, that from bidding them ten plagues of Egypt I restrain -
Domine, da mihi aquam . . .

Who are these monstrous villains, whom we accuse and blame?
The thought of which makes one shudder; who kill, rape and maim?
- Manifold are their faces, and diverse is their aim,
Some kill for the land and power or their revenge proclaim,
But those who kill little children in their unbridled lust
It's hardest to forgive; so, help me, O Merciful and Just
Domine, da mihi aquam . . .

You ask me - are they humans? And who have reared them?
- Their parents, brother, mass media, brother, a Godless team . . .
Our leaders, brother, our clergy, brother, and teachers, too,
They all corrupt our youngsters, poison their minds and souls,
We both are also guilty, for we malice couldn't face,
So, let's pray together, brother, for God's cleansing grace:
Domine, da mihi aquam . . .

Slowly creeps on evil, yet progressively it creeps,
Until it has one's body and soul in its mighty grip,
It starts as 'personal freedom', and 'progress', and the rest,
Then lust comes, drugs, and greed, and hatred at its worst.
So, that we could discern it, and in the bud it thwart,
Let's pray to our Lord Jesus in these familiar words:
Domine, da mihi aquam . . .

Barbara J Niemienionek-Lindsay

Long Boats

Long boats; lingering in lethargic
undulations placidly plashing
wet timber gates and meshes of weed
Awakening in the waving wake
duck-bobbing drake honks and dabbles
quietly in the brimming mead

Unassuming intrusions in the
filmy element proceed in
chuntering diesel-thrumming ease
By waving towpath people
landlocked on the florid
trail where equus used to wheeze

Painted coach-work pin-striped
in abundant flora, Dutch dancers
clogged, church-window bright and sheer
Weave about the wanderers' delft
domicile, utensils, cans; all brass
bedecked, an ornamental pier

Varnished in vernacular river
culture augmented in ropes and
trinkets round panelling packed
With cabinets and crevices
all-purposeful arranged in
Noah's ageing timbers, cracked

Serenity and adventure in
plimsolls squeaks a
saturation of blithe leisure
Bargees' hardships long forgot
in tiller-gripped meanderings
on serenaded streets with full Venetian measure

Alex Oliver

Unflattering portrait rings all too true

1 Boris Yeltsin has these muches in common with Benjamin Disraeli

the rings
the portrait
the too
the unflattering

2 In his Russia nothing is true, all is imaginable

3 Nobody knows the roubles he's seen

Steve Edgell

Beauty Rarely Seen

Down the dusty footpath,
In and out the trees,
Up and over hillocks,
Flying in the breeze.

Watching swallows darting
Round and round and round.
Losing soggy footholds
In the sodden ground.

Reaching ever upwards,
Grasping every rock.
Gazing over landscapes;
Simply taking stock.

Coming down to earth again,
Noticing the green
And gold and brown and grey and black;
Beauty rarely seen.

Running through the flying grass;
Tossing every step.
Turning at another's smile,
Wanting this to keep.

Finding now a harder way,
Different conversation:
Talk of end and talk of rest,
Reaching destination.

Aching limbs, but spirits high.
Coming into view:
See two bridges over hill,
Nearly there, we two.

A bench, a pool and water clear,
A very glad reaction.
The two of us gaze skywards
With a sense of satisfaction.

Ziggy Whitehead

Arkitecture

Before the deluge surged and swelled
and clapped its belly onto their universe,
she built diligently
with the moon as her overseer
against the undoing.

Month followed month
of estimated escape;
sacrificed fleshy fingers
for hammer and nail.
Fitted plank upon plank.
Pitted element against element.
Until finally the ark.

Then the tumble
of rum-blind thunder
rolled under rains.
Rhythmic refrains arose
as he refused rescue.

Day after day now
she longs for delivering dove
and dreams of endless deserts.

Out here
he washes over her
and there is too much drowning.

Indeed, she is the sea itself
trapped as a conch shell
in ocean echo.

With the word
she must drag the water
in the beginning.

Carol Margaret Davison

Hanging

What hangs on that wall is an exact and needed
Choice: the photograph of Sienese
Housetops with windows ajar into the past;
Ravenna mosaics like still visible light
From an extinguished star; the octagonal church
Where I was caught in a downpour of grace.

They are not there for recollection.
Forgetting is not the enemy, but neglect,
Not looking after what makes us ourselves.
Dead memories rot. In case I do not smell
My own decay drifting down time, that wall
Is there to tell whether I am alive.

Michael Parsons

Sounds

Waking in the dark to heavy rain,
Remembering a narrow
Crooked house. Stark, part stone,
Part wood it stood, jutting
Above the street below
Like a prow of a ship.

A small girl listening
To footsteps as they pass beneath,
Wondering whose they are?
Walking in the rain, lulling her to sleep.

Hears the foghorn calling in the night,
The lighthouse beam bathes her window,
Washes her wall white.

The sea, a giant heartbeat,
Pounds the beach, covers
The rock-pools feet, swirls
Round limpet shells, swells
Sucking in pebbles, spews them out.

Waking in the dark, no foghorn
But the call of owls.
No lighthouse, but moonshine still
Bathes wall and windowsill, no
Footsteps, save those of rutting deer.
Wind rustling leaves,
Sea exchanged for woods, but the same
Sound, the same sweet sound,
Heavy falling rain.

Mary Blake

Saving the Phenomena

Something about a widening gyre
he thinks, brooding over the calendar. 'Will you be
free, darling, on the . . . ?' Her movements
seem less predictable now,
though there's no reason to suspect . . .

She leaves for the theatre, looking radiant and wavier.
What causes such eccentric
behaviour? He asks himself, taking a seat in the gods.
He trains his telescope on a galaxy -

That's odd - that satellite . . . But a solid phalanx
of stars, theatrical luminaries,
passes between them.

Some kind of occultation
seems to have taken place.
Inexplicable, unless . . .

Now epicycles are wheeled on, not before time,
and - yes - they will do. The paradigm
can remain pragmatically unaltered:

any devoted theatregoer
would appear to describe the same erratic orbit.
No crisis, then; no loss of face.
But for all his positivism,
one explanation begins to feel truer -

there's another planet out there.

Penny McCarthy

The Breakdown

How I was in pain that clammy, bleak, grey winter
With a pain I could not share,
Pain of the soul that freezes the flesh,
When you brushed my cheek gently,
Light as a vapour that softly speaks in tender fragrance;
Yet I would not take tenderness
Held out to me on waiting arms of expectation.
But we made love. Panting, tense, cheerless, damp,
My flesh did mingle with your soft, eternal warmth
In that dark corner away from the window
Where winter sun beamed his diamond light upon your emerald floors
And brightened just the tip of my shoes.
Yes we made love; and when the pleasure pierced the agony,
The bullet burst the flesh,
I merely stood,
Concealed myself, zipped my fly and took my pain away
Through the unlocked door into the darkness of the outer room
Where night winds hissed in gloomy whispers through the cracks,
Too filled with self unbegotten to even care
Now two lost souls stumbled, blinded there,
Breathing in pain and tears.

Edgar Wyatt Stephens

Untitled

Eventually the exorcist came,
With his innate magic,
And due ceremony,
And blessed water in a plastic bottle,
To cleanse this contaminated place,
Soiled by lurking irreverent spirits,
That excrete upon the alter,
And merrily foul symbols of our faith.
All the corners of this place contain
An accumulated dust of heresy,
Where virus breed in rusting cans,
And bacteria fight their microscopic wars
Amid the jungled architecture of cigarette butts.
Yes, it's very dirty here,
A fetid atmosphere of lowered expectations.
Infection disintegrates matter,
The envelope of mind.
Even the devil, with his exultation of evil,
Seldom visits.

So the exorcist came,
Bringing his blunt instruments of salvation,
And we helped with appropriate gestures
Of respect, humility, and shame,
And uncovered,
And discovered,
An acceptance of evil.

Anita Curtis

Christmas Tree

Star
Brightly shine
Let nothing mar
This designer pine
Let there be no bar
To elegant sweep of line
No colourful clutter to jar
On chaste garlands that entwine
Cold branches, free of doll or toy car
For childhood's delight offer no sign
Nothing to make little children cry, 'Ah!'
Appeal only to those whose taste is fine.

Yet shrilling from afar
Is a small child's whine
To come near the star.

Vera Charles

The Flag

From distant shorelines came the flag now waved
With promises well-weaved into the cloth
And for two hundred years the Brits have raved
But now some locals ache to show their wrath.
Oz has the colour green 'longside the gold
Suits well the eye, a most delightful hue
The politicians have the wind from old
Post them a vote and it will fly true blue.
Yet there are tintings more in this brown land
A nature scene for forty thousand years
First, make the new *One Nation Act* real grand
So that *The Dreamtime* proves to have no fears.
  Whatever runs up on a new-flag pole
  The Blacks and Whites need have an equal role.

Caswell Newton

Slip of a Thing

Slip of a thing
Waiting for the bus
You twitch a cigarette
In nervous fingers,
Your brittle laugh with friends
Contains no joy.
Sad to see
Inherent lovely spring
Appear a surly February.
What is the stress
That makes you so?
Does no-one care?
I do.

John Wedge

Sandcastles

It took about twenty minutes to build,
Twenty minutes of steady labour -
Digging and filling, and patting flat,
Overturning, carefully, easing out -
Five round towers and an outer moat,
Limpet shells to prick out the parapet;
Only the lack
Of a scarlet flag
Made your castle short of perfection.

But, while you worked, the sea was creeping
Down through the trenches between the rocks,
Flicking the half-dried seaweeds free -
Twitching dull, brown fingers to shining life.
One moment the moat filled, and then emptied again,
Before a white cliff broke on the barbican.
You shrieked to see
It wash away,
Then ran to build another in the sands.

Fiona Stafford

Each to Each (the Merman Answers)

> *The knife trembled in the Little Mermaid's hand, but then she threw it far out into the sea . . . Once more she looked upon the Prince with dying eyes, then threw herself from the vessel and felt her body dissolving into foam.*
>
> *Hans Anderson - The Little Mermaid*

You may have been the youngest
but you were the bravest -
your fishtail flicking through coral,
the fastest and the slickest.
Then, as the dry-world moon
pierced our underwater forest,
licking the gain shells, the amber,
silvering the sand;
in the last hour before slumber,
on those nights, I would sing for you.

Black day - I lured a ship onto the rocks
with my deep song. Hot head! Rusher-in!
Who would not let that clumsy bi-ped drown,
nor leave him breathe his stale air alone,
but followed him back to his arid land
on gross white stumps, tongue-tied,
dancing on needles, red-hot knives;
trading your tail for the chance of a soul.
I mourn, coming as close as I dare,
and on quiet nights, I sing for you.

Lost for words, you couldn't tell him
that your clear blood was royal as his.
One last hope . . . but you flung the knife,
shining an instant, into the reddening sea.
I cannot even say you died -
soulless spume on a surface tide.
Mermen, remember, have no tears.

It doesn't mean a thing to you
but I shall live three hundred years
and each night, I shall sing for you.

Susan Kelly

Hymn to Priapus

Old wooden god in the rose-bed,
How does your garden grow?
How do you hold your hard thought
When the winds blow?

Is it a close, lascivious dream
Of youth in bloom and leaf?
Or a deep winter's vigil, a long
Standing grief?

Let Aeolus tame the winds, friend,
Let country cuckoos sing,
Let hamadryads lightly run
Through wanton Spring,

Let flowers dance, let April pour
Libations on the grass;
And let us know your vigour - though
We die, alas.

Humphrey Clucas

Hail the Heretic Lover

Hail the heretic lover who upon my woman descends,
Sapping my mind, my humanity, upon which my person depends.
Hard won seeds of sanity dispersed with seeds of hell;
Seeking strength in solitude, moments when I dwell.

Rosalyn Carr

On Meon Hill

My Meon, my earthy thumb
stubbed in the heart of Avon's valley -
a plateau's fist. We sit
on its knuckle, scan the countryside
laid out like a model of my life.
I point to the landmarks that defined me
from a vantage point that has moved on,
but shadowed by them.

I feel childlike in your company -
you inhabit landscapes of feeling
I cannot understand, or leave just yet.
But the warm breezes of fascination
are carrying me - up, high and away.
Watch me rise, a kite
on your string.
Cut the thread - release my feathered
heart, sever my ties.

And I am the hawk
rising on a thermal, solitary,
looking down on you,
too still to swoop on. I will fly
on the dark wings of love -
soar into the sun.
Watch me closely:
I eclipse the light, disappear,
then, careering down,
come screaming in the night
to make you tender, pray;
to make you vulnerable again.

Damian Furniss

Searching For Something of Sentimental Value

Walking
And arguing with fear,
Along the barren track of a blank day,
A story begins to form
Which marks each step as a fall
And notes each thought as desire.
Fixed by movement scenes are formed,
Buildings once overgrown with decay
Develop a history beyond their brick,
Writing a history of time recreated.
People are formed and develop character
Worn with the pride of innocence,
Not self created, but born into a stream of tradition.
Stiffened by a backbone of boredom
The foot falls and shatters a complex of memories,
Yet remains yoked to the story
With the passionate attachment of a traveller
Hoping to finding the sublime in the species of simplicity
Turning an epigram, twisted to purpose,
Or praying formed phrases into suitable icons.
Walking
And arguing with fear
Passing the time and recreating the tale.

Ian Webster

Portrait Group by James Cowie

I came upon your faces for the second time.
The first also in Edinburgh.
But this time the crowds swarmed around you.
Ah . . . yes! Festival '93!
The Line of Tradition
And what a draughtsman.
Your linear, hard-edged figures greeted me
and drew me into their mind and landscapes.
I won't forget the pink blazer
the decorated tablecloth
the apples akin to Cézanne
the background draperies
and those faces

distanced
in a psychological landscape of Cuminestown.

You were isolated from the modern mainstream.
A Scottish painter
A surrealist before we even knew the name.
Here you were reliving summer childhood
the innocence and timelessness
of a loon in Kincardineshire.

Leaving the classroom
you never forgot your pupils, your models
or your training of Quattrocento Italian art -
the objective line and colour.

I am happy to see the group again
and wish I had been part of it.

Karen M C Meikle

A Poem for Lovers in Leap Year

The places where the land runs out and
                                                            falls
into the sea;

where sands of time under limestone
                                                         cliffs
slip downward endlessly;

where clouds uncouple and drift on
                                                     by
in blithe vapidity;

where you are alone and I am al-
                                              one
and we're not just you and me;

these are the places, these are the laces
these are the aces we can
                                        be.

Robert Stradling

Thanks for Coming

What is sex, if, full of woe,
I do not come and then you go?
One contrives the bodies' meeting
to find fulfilment far too fleeting
to know if that was really *it.*
Was that all? Or just a bit?

The flesh that lures is then found wanting
during all this sweat and panting,
wrestling, struggling, seething, slopping.
Is there more? Oh, God, he's stopping.
Look, cut out head, give cunt its share.
You're always thinking, always there;
watching all the rest at work;
mocking antics with a smirk.

Oh yes! Oh yes! That's gorgeous, really.
Yes. Yes, I came. Well . . . almost . . . nearly.

It's not your fault; mine, of course.
No, I'm not crying; merely hoarse
from making gasps orgasmic-seeming
while my brain was wildly teeming.
Yes! You're fantastic! Honest. Yes.
Perfect lover. More or less.

Oh shit. I might go mad instead
and sleep with apples in my bed.

Liz Adamson

Moon Child

All her life she'd been floating
On a subfusc lake,
A meadow brown child carrying
Unshared dreams in deep-set pockets.
Grown in the skin of a pearl,
A seamless shell of gossamer
Wound tight to keep the world out.
Pale, full-blown moon drifting
On a juvenile sea
To a willow pattern school
Somewhere in Middle England.

Always alone, thinking words,
Writing thoughts, poet
Consecrated to the Pole star.
Hyperbole was her comfort.
Original sin's passport
Prized open her mouth to utter
Mea maxima culpa.
Sweet and low, dark and soft
In a light and hard land
Cast a bitter after-birth
On fresh perfume amongst thorns.

Later her body was found
Drowned in a viridian swamp,
Swollen with invisibility,
A faraway smile on her lips.

Helen Luson

Culture Shock

She was taught to count petals
as connotations of affections
positive from negative
his third person taking
precedence over her first,
his worst better than her best,
her request
too demanding
he commanding
I will . . . *and she does.*

She is expected to retain
the required and admired
obsession by possession
her humility attracting
a greater measure
of pain than pleasure
less she begin to address
her own essential
latent potential
I can't . . . and he agrees.

She has learnt not to expect
the notion of devotion
dedication by affirmation
he may play away
her dried blossom eyes
overlooking his games without aims
no more rebuking
with raised voices
and ultimate choices
he begs . . . and she leaves.

Elaine Hogan

Lost Love

My lovely daughter, believe me I've tried,
I've often tried,
to let you know,
how much,
I really love you.

For three long weeks,
You watched me suffering in pain.
'It's my 13th birthday, remember . . .'
you whisper softly in my ear.

I know I've left it far too late,
to tell you what you mean to me.
I'm dying now . . .
My breathing's shallower.
A dark and silent grave, my destiny.

You and I are separating, forever
No more to see,
your loving, smiling face.

Patricia McAllister

For Edith Sitwell

What is my wing now but the heavy load
Of heaven upon a sinner's shoulder?
A leaf for laughter would fare far better,
Dancing for pipers, ripe along the road.

Adam chose names from a forest Babel.
Years took exile where his beasts had trodden.
Prophets are flying above the midden.
I have waved them homeward with my shovel.

Surely the guilt I seek shall judge me soon,
And the one familiar witness worship
The disappearing God, the end of light.
Then on the path of rupee or doubloon
A stranger invites me to the dark ship
And takes my sin and dries it till it's white.

Peter Christensen

Borders

Borders made of weeds, a patch of earth,
    soon it will be park-like in her eyes,
    dappled lawns and summer-soft blue skies.
Imagination conjures up the turf
and bud-strewn roses waiting to give birth,
    foxgloves kissed by dipping butterflies
            in borders.

The vision dulled through winter's quelling gloom,
    backache of a gardener pulling weeds.
    Springtime and the sowing of the seeds.
Herbaceous flowers surging into bloom
            in borders.

Valerie Thame

Renovation

Unwilling to take notice
We let the place decay.
Through loving it, we lost it
And saw things fall away.
Afraid, perhaps, that over-anxious care
Wreaks havoc worse than weather's constant wear.

Another winter's rage would disengage
Too many ancient slates and weary walls.
Save it we must but when at last we're through
Our home must still remain the one we knew.

That if the ones that built it
Four hundred years ago
To last as long as man may need
A lovely place to go
Should find, as shades, they wander
Into our present day;
Find grim and graceless buildings
Where once sweet pastures lay;
Find concrete cities choking
The earth, the air, the skies,
Still here there will be something
That they can recognise.

Frances Classon

Punting in Cambridge During Easter Vacation

Aimless as goldfish, the tourists gawp and drift
from one spot to another, pausing to lift
their cameras in the direction of some
tower, garden, bridge, monument. They have come
here from the ends of the earth: Nagasaki,
Iowa, Melbourne; now they are watching me.
A duffer afloat, I struggle with the pole
of my punt - a craft that seems to have a soul,
and a rebellious one. Drifting, it slows, spins,
nudges the bank, drifts again. Someone begins
to titter. A finger points. Intent eyes peer
into viewfinders. Shutters click. A small cheer
goes up as I regain control, my mishaps
recorded for a score of holiday snaps.

Arthur McHugh

Grave Robbers

The crows,
Encloaked in black.
The cloth conceals the dancing cadavers.
The crows,
The chattering, shrieking, cackling crows,
Bent and twisted, like mad shadows -
Of death.

The worms,
They hop greedily round them,
Their beaks like missiles -
Harpooning the tender skin,
Then fly, wavering - Filled to surfeit from the rich nutrition within.

Michael Stewart

The Disappearance of a Flint-Hoard

The hottest night,

with a mind

emulsified

by market forces

stirring

the bedroom curtains

with facets

of the moon.

James Revenant

Blackbird

In the liquid engineering of the dawn
an oily overalled mechanic
dips his black can
again, again,
fine tuning the
amazing green technology of lawn.

Peter Wallis

Death Restores Control

After ten minutes sleep or ten hours
There is no difference in the abstract
Existence of this father, son or holy
Ghost of a man. He pulls the life from
His half crucified body and lights the
Distilled brain.

The high street shines, taxis head off
Towards places called home. Club Nova
Pours youth downstairs, down drains into
strange affairs. Drunks dispute a fare.
Law and order restores control.

Friday night, Tuesday night there all the same
Reality stinks, he's glad of his abstract dream
No complications, no comprehension's little apprehensions.

Lovers embrace in another doorway
'The night belongs to lovers'
Clutching his figure of Christ
He concludes.

Samuel McCarter

Mind - the Magnolia

Within the gardens of my mind
Tight-cornered near the utmost hedge
I watch its pristine blooms
Aim tips aloft, unleafed, springing into spring.

Gently tuned to the universe
Each open heart cranes upwards
Gathering thought drifts, draining softest pink
From the sunset and capturing rainbows.

Else the flowers fade without them
The weighty outspread leaves perfect the marriage
Easing their branches
To catch the low-pitched sounds.

Summered by darting bees, peppered with pollen
Blossoms peak - their life complete
The breeze they once withstood
Snatches mottled petals to fall like outused words.

Sodden with weeping, the heavy leaves follow
Spread-eagled to the ground - flat untidy
And deepening dung coloured
Rot in soggy heap.

Standing still time - bare, snappy and stick-brown
Ready for snow . . . but wait . . . well wrapped
The honed new buds arise in fixed remembered shapes
Close-holding cold memories, till coaxed by sun
They cheek the chink-stretched light
And stretch against the confines of my head.

Norma Rhys-Davies

Magic Carpet

Sitting cross-legged, bending forwards
the child learns the pattern,
places threads,
In, out; red, yellow, blue.

Twenty threads to the inch,
In, out; red, yellow, blue.

Trellised leaves grow.
In, out; red, yellow, blue.

The sun glares on the tin roof,
sweat gleams on brown skin,
flies buzz unnoticed.
In, out; red, yellow, blue.

Paradise peacocks grow.
In, out; red, yellow, blue.

Dreams fly unseen,
Cool fountains glisten,
Parasols dance above dark heads,
Deep shadows form cool pools.
In, out; ruby, gold, azure.

Trellised gardens flower.
In, out; ruby, gold, azure.

Twenty threads to the inch.
In, out; ruby, gold, azure.

The carpet lies on the marble floor,
praised by princes,
dreamt by a child.
In, out; red, yellow, blue.

Elisabeth Norton

A Life

I'm young and standing on the brink.
Tell me: Will I simply sink?
Or will I play a brilliant game
and reach astounding heights of fame?
Perhaps it's youth that keeps me yearning -
wanting more from life than earning.
Given age, I'll give up hope;
and quite content, I'll simply cope.
But now, at life's beginning still,
I'm free to dread or dream at will.

I've reached the middle of the stream
and left the days of dread and dream.
My age ahead, my youth behind,
I'm busy at the daily grind.
A world of dull suburban houses!
Still, I've got the best of spouses.
Children too - but growing fast
and proving patterns never last.
The future looms; and soon I'll miss
this drab today as years of bliss.

Wilting now, and widowed too,
now I've nothing left to do.
My children grown, my pension small,
what's been the purpose of it all?
Was the object of this life
the happiness of man and wife?
Or was its point to be of use
to genes concerned to reproduce?
Or was I born to somehow find
a purpose of a higher kind?

R G S Sprigge

Mother Nature - Father Time

A loving couple struggle in the wave of modern life.
Mother Nature cradles the Earth in her arms.
Skies torn,
Trees cut down,
Babies born in a world of warring eruption and mindless corruption.
Madness runs rife in the wave of modern life.
Mother Nature shakes her head and begins to weep.

Father Time sees his wife in distress,
And holds her tightly to his breast.
Trying to comfort her growing sorrow, he knows his problems
are not faraway.

The clock of Life ticks far too fast,
Today and tomorrow plunge into the past.
People seem so busy working nine till five,
Overtime and extra time, working time to stay alive.
And Father Time struggles, but manages to survive.
A loving couple,
A husband and wife,
Drowning in the wave of modern life.

Darren Powell

Contemporaries

Tony - I dragged him from the calculus
Around the links - is in *Who's Who*
He got his Nobel at the court of Vasa;
David, youngest of the Bank House three
(Our predecessors in old Theo's time)
Could name the key of the church bell
About as soon as he could talk
Is now Sir David and conducts the Proms;
Elspeth, of those beach picnics -
How the damp trunks of shyness clung!
Was tack-sharp at ten, alert for material
Are we transmuted in her bitchy works?
Geoffrey the owl, who never put a foot
Wrong at school, got Environment
In the last Tory government but one.
Have they time now to remember
The harbour, familiar in the crook
Of shore and headland, the cliffs
Weighted with Edwardian hotels
Empty at Christmas for our parties?
What *was* it in the air or soil
At the end of that axed branch line?
The daily air is thick with noise
Of those who made it, one way or another
But these, no louder, are distinct
They put my landscape in the reference books
Though we grumbled when our parents made us meet.

John Hewish

Villanelle: The Jigsaw

A jigsaw vast the Master made
and sent it down to earth,
a vivid cavalcade was laid

an intricately wrought brocade
of joy and precious worth.
A jigsaw vast the Master made

with colours that shall never fade;
of richness there's no dearth.
A vivid cavalcade was laid,

its jewels ceaselessly cascade
upon a heedless earth.
A jigsaw vast the Master made,

a never-ending rich parade
to please his creatures on the earth
a vivid cavalcade was laid.

Our grateful thanks are oft delayed
for glory of such heavenly birth.
A jigsaw vast the Master made,
a vivid cavalcade was laid.

Geraldine Squires

He Chose to Part

Hence were thee; now get thee hence once more
Foul failings, called emotions.
Crowd of false devotions
Of two nectar lips;
Succumbing to another's sips,
As he would drink of the well thee would adore.

Lament not, heart: for was thy flinted edge did cleave
That thin and fragile rope
Of the well's pail of hope,
And love, filled to the brink;
For thee, at any time to drink
Or bathe a troubled brow: 'fore thee chose to leave.

Ache now, gut: and wear a painèd cloak
About thine empty form:
Sheltered not, the storm
Of deserved and unrelenting guilt,
For razed devotion another built:
And upon each found, fond memory: have thee choke.

Michael P Andrews

Panic Attack?

That anonymity of early morning in the city. Outlook black.
There had been pressure before when you felt as if you
were going to crack.
It must have been around two o'clock. Confrontation. Sudden shock.

'Right Jimmy. Money. The lot. Give. And quick. OK?'

You felt real sick and you felt yourself tighten, shudder and shake.

Your first impulse was to turn and run but when he produced a gun -
Dummy one or not - you didn't and couldn't. Not when you're faced
With something so frightening, barbaric and ignorant. What a
predicament.
Right in the shit, they call it.

OK, you say, gesturing, wait a minute, and you stuck your
hand into your
Anorak-pocket just as if you were going for your wallet. It was a real
Pregnant moment as you'd almost forgotten that unknown to
your wee wife
You carried a knife to protect your life.

Then, blood coursing up into your brain, like a madman you went
for the cunt
Stabbing and ripping with manic delight into the bastard's fat gut as
You heard him gasp, gag and moan, then issue a wet and
skittery huge fart.
And you too so humane and intelligent.

Like going through the motions. Like a dream, everything
somehow so distant.

But then through a red mist you withdrew the knife with a
sickening twist
And like a lump of meat the bastard fell back against the
grafittied wall.

Who was now the criminal you heard yourself yell. Who is fucking ill?
You who'd always fought for the downtrodden lumpen proletariat.
You can hardly believe it.

Some sleeping giant. More like an ignorant ant. Thank Christ
it was dark.
Sick. Distressed. Paranoiac. You got off your mark over
the fence and
Down through the silent park. Self-defence the best method
of attack?

Thoughts and emotions uneven you chuck the fucking weapon
into the Kelvin.

Home again. No one is in. You search for any incriminating
stain. None.
You open a can, turn on the television and switch off the phone.
No dream.
It's real. A not so cool kill. Imminent that silent scream. Soul in hell.
And prison will be no heaven.

Jack Withers

A Wayside Halt: Genolier

Remembering, among others, Keats again;
these names never leave my side. Here
is a theme with a new refrain.

The mountain train glides to a halt
past citron glades and knee-high grass,
the uncreased blue of sky an open vault.

You have walked today the lavender paths,
scented the vineyards' bounty, traced
skylarks and butterflies in swirling dance.

Remembering, among others, Keats in constant flight
from his inexorable doom: time pursues us -
yet leaves her favours within sight.

Yvonne Gunawardena

The User

The old man on the ferry
talks.
His wife
neither encourages him nor says
Belt up.

He is a sailing man.
His subject is the Junior Offshore Group.

Although he's audible
his mouth stays shut.
He's shaping some account,
needing for this
the silent presence of his wife
who gives no sign of having heard
a single word.

And yet if she, who must know this by heart,
weren't there,
this rubbish said through lip-screened teeth
wouldn't escape to offend
the just less innocent integument of air.

P S Joll

Lovely Sara

I've heard the moon whispering to the stars
About your beauty about your olive eyes
One lost its way, one fells in your universe,
but another still fading away,
Here it dies.
They all swore that no one would shine again,
no one would rise!
Since your radiant face shining in size.
They all swore to remain in hiding and be disguised,
Since you're still shining on them,
They're all amazed.
I've heard the spring-like waters singing your name
praising your beauty, praising your fame,
The lyrics were simple repeating the same,
Oh lovely Sara! in look and name.
I've seen the nightingale singing in cage,
I've seen the parrot in wild in rage,
Picking minty leaves and sage,
shouting and shouting without blame.
I've seen the sun setting down in shyness,
For your undeclared title your highness,
You're a princess of joy, smile, and finesse,
You baby-sit the elder, the young and the baby-boy.
Your innocent look your childish nose,
Your ringy mouth, your cheeks in rose,
Your strawberry lips, your tongue in pose,
They all in place like a pretty toy.
Your tar oiled hair,
Your skin is fair,
My sight is blur,
I've lost it boy!
Your thighs and lips,
Your kiss and tips,
Your bosom and hips,
Are you an attraction or a divine decoy?
Your scruffy hair is a blossomed flower,

showing its petals higher and lower,
indicating directions like a tower.

Abder

Road Wallah

Now the roads are different:
They pass not along the lake,
Nor do they skirt the mountain base,
Nor dribble into desecrated ruins,
Nor patchwork the desert lace
Strewn between strange tribes
(Thickened into textures
Of disease, and rites, and bribes).

These roads are not as they are
Crumbled mud-baked tracks
Where parrots, men and camels
Rise threadbare from the cracks.

These roads incline to hamlets,
Neat, squared, and with green,
Where passers-by are 'county'
Whose feet are never seen.
The village clock is ancient,
Its trust chimes out each hour,
And where the coffee morning hums
Among the knitted vests,
Whose cast-off thoughts
For far-off lands
Solve charity's stiff tests.

The talk idles into headlines,
It dare not reach below;
And mouths are full of cake crumbs,
And lies as white as snow.

They've heard that times are tricky
In way off Kathmandu
And grimly are determined
To get the woollies through.

Michael Deane-White

Untitled

As beauty, heart in her mouth, yields her up,
black tongues tisk-tisk from inscrutable dials.
A plucked string breaks at the height of the dance,
and one piercing dissonance freezes all smiles.

Pink autumn snows from the spring cherry trees;
a cold air mass bears down on rapt boys and girls.
Our hands touched once, barely relayed their warmth,
while the kalpas roll away, spilt ropes of pearls.

Paul Mackintosh

Entry in a New Diary

Nothing much happened today;
the weather cyclonic, cold and grey
with a taste of coal-smoke in the wind.
I walked in a ramshackle wood and remarked
- how nettles thrive where men discard their rubbish;
last year's brittle stems bleached by frost
and now, by the prevaricating winds, criss-crossed;
this year's brood was busy hatching out of rusting metal:
- how a broken bed discomforted the uneasy furniture of earth;
(the silent choir of heaven was otherwise engaged):
- how from a black holly tree a pigeon beat
a maladroit retreat
and startled scuffling blackbirds from the bracken:
- how in a neat circle at the wood's still centre
a chestnut tree had shed its leaves,
rust-brown beside the pale plague-spotted sycamore,
some transfixed by two-inch bluebell spikes.

Catkins of alder small and hard
but a sign of purplish leaf on elder and woodbine
and then, by the stream, I saw a wren
creep like a mouse across great cushions
of emerald golden saxifrage:
and so I came home
where I should be content this year to say
nothing much happened every day.

Michael Paffard

Green Fuse

When within me something twists or
Snaps, when envy, loneliness or
Fire begins to flow, first mild
Beneath my ribs then throbbing through
My chest, when spirits of the desert
Bottled in my brain, and strangers
Torn from breathless, sunstruck plains
Slow start to pound about my heart,
When every muscle of my soul
Spits bile, shouts silent anguish of its
Own, and every fragment of my
Self seethes hate and hot despair,

Then, oh my land, then do I dream of thee,
And bathe me in cool waters from the hills,
And stand where herons watch, and soar beyond
The green, grey, silent crags that rest below;
Then do I sit beside the furthest rock,
And breath white spray, tossed from the boundless sea.

Gideon Lester

Destiny's Song

The black turbulence
of tomorrow's form taking shape
transcending today's swift progression
of non-permanent echo.

Heal world; I say.
The shouts of distant voices
can only be the sound
of my own internal voice.

There is so much to do.
The struggle develops
as two roads manifest their imposing,
stark presence.

Only through the existence of thought
can the leaves,
the remnants
be gathered and burnt
to generate a thick, hard, sick
but fresh suffocating smoulder
To fashion the path.

James Neophytou

Heroes

What are those purple, black, scarlet, white and blue fairy lights twinkling and glistening on the yellow and mauve daisy heads swaying in the autumnal sunlight? They are red admiral butterflies, migrants from the north journeying towards the tempestuous grounds that reek with the life of the blazing sunshine and the death from the chilly blasts of night.

But still they come in droves, hordes of colourful insects gliding through the air, alighting on the flowers, displaying their medallion wings, closing them to show darker shades of red, black, brown purple and grey that defile their royalty regaled on the feast of death.

For by morning, they are all dead; fallen petals of shimmering, fragile beauty littering and enriching the first brown leaves which already cover the garden path.

And yet there are other red admirals migrants fluttering splendidly over their dead comrades. How their multicoloured wings quiver in the cruel sunshine! Soft, silken, tremulous, painted threads thriving on the nectar following their fallen companions to majestic glory and death.

It's the battle cry of man. Fight valiantly, show your pageantry, feast, surrender and die.

J T Willans

The Graveyard of Names

They stood in the shadow beneath the wall,
Archilochus, Acamas, Hyrtacydes,
Their war-cries strangled; words forestalled
Or lost in dust; and comrades' calls
Hung in unanswered air or drifted across the seas
And that was all.
Their blades cracked; horses stood half dead with sweat;
Their topless towers were riddled with disease;
And enemy faces under the bronze masks
Glowed black; in battle met
A million times, and names unknown as yet,
For what are names now?
Fight them one by one - that is the task
And there's an end.
(But under the bronze mask
They seem so similar, the foe, the friend)
And as for her;
A creasing face which showed some beauty then,
If not as was once famed -
We do not fight for her, nor for that day
When the white foam brought her in
But only for today.
What was her name?

And at last, when they rent those towers from side to side,
And the dust rose, and the flames,
Around the graveyard of names,
A few words might have been gasped
(The spirit fleeing the clenched teeth)
And carried along the breeze
To the poet who listened and ambushed them like a thief.

C L C Black

Zen and the Feral Shadows of Dusk

Life is like a journey
made in spring it is soon
over and forgotten - the only
consolation no trace of one's

vileness will ever remain
both good and evil return
to the original void the human
moment a leaf falling to a burn

the feral shadows of dusk all
ask one question did we live
according to our nature's law
or simply make a mess of our life

Francis Gallagher

Deltics 1965-81

You don't know how it feels,
the jiggling sensation waist downwards,
knowing you're being pulled by Lorna Doone.

Nothing compares to the smooth curve of windows
and six cylinders beneath bolted blue.
Shunting up behind me their breath steams;
pistons pump against the metal sweating blebs;
I shut my notebook and go home to bed.

I cried when they scrapped that class.
They guillotined The Earl of Westmorland's rear;
his spent grease guttered across the sweltering yard.
Now I dream of flying over humming sheds
and oiling engines, worrying whether it's correct
to scribble them down without being whole.

On the platform of awful pies,
buttocks sogged on a ribbed pack-up seat
I flask and muse, what if stars aren't stars,
but holes in black bodywork through
to a blaze of whistles where 55's go?

Antony Rowland

The Cuckoo and the Bridal Wreath

She was married without the brides'
arching posy in trembling hands.
She had a baby in the secret world
of her husband's bed.

She carried her hunched shoulders
into twenty, a discomforted cuckoo.
Now she's sent a Valentine, the offer
of a heart and a kiss:

now she dresses to inflame her blush
and her smile, her straightened back
bending only to share a confidence
with the man that she has chosen

to re-live with, the whole downward
branching stem of tiny petals
with brown microdot freckles.

Ralph Hancock

The Wino

City streets etched on vermilion face
From a thousand falls, blood-shot eyes,
Soul mirror reflecting hell, broken nose,
Unremembered punch-ups. Smells of the gutter,
Urine and other bodily functions.

Home, is sometimes a large cardboard box,
In a rat infested basement, in a derelict building.
Fitful sleep is ended each morning by the
Shakes, sickness, vomit and paranoia, as the
Body demands the fiery fuel. Going forth
To face a cold sober humanity, and a
Thousand cold sober refusals begging a coin,
Which will gain admittance to the
Dream world of the full bottle.

First gulp of the fiery fuel stops
The shakes, sickness, vomit and paranoia,
As it circulates through the channels
Of the body, warming the very cockles of
The heart. The full bottle is the shield
Against the cold logic of life's reality.

The fiery fuel, coursing its merry way through
The channels of the body, causes a personality
Change, the bodily functions are the functions
Of an infant, but there is no one to
Change the clothes, wash and powder the
Body, no one to prepare the bottle, to soothe
The anguished cry in the night.

Over the unrecorded years the fiery fuel
Burns out the body and death comes in a
Fitful sleep in a rat infested basement,
In some derelict building.

Gerard Kenny

A Sestina to the Bird of Paradise

Enrobed in scarlet, brilliant blazing bird
    With eagle' strength, a child of sacred fire,
She sounds a cry that is forever heard.
    Consumed in Self-lit flames she does aspire,
Ascending from her pyre, to show to all the world
    Herself from death, reborn! Each man she does inspire.

In ancient times this Wonder did inspire.
    From Heliopolis there flew this fabled bird
To reach the Sun, the lamplight of our world,
    And immolating in this mystic fire
New Being rose out of ashes. So aspire
    To see new Life from Death. These words were heard.

When this Egyptian legend first was heard
    The daring thought was one that did inspire
Everyman, who now has right to so aspire,
    Because of the bold example of this splendid bird;
And if he falls upon the sacrificial fire
    He would emerge as Victor of his World.

This paragon is thus a symbol to our world
    Proclaiming news that everywhere is heard
Setting the wooden minds of men on fire,
    The deathless spirit mocks at death. Inspire!
Thanks to the valour of this courageous bird
    The soul of man, can to an afterlife aspire.

Now peoples of all lands may well aspire
    To reach a peak of hope in an unhelpful world
And follow the flight of virtue set by this beloved bird.
    So sound the golden trumpet to be heard,
Men know this transformation can inspire
    To be born again from sacramental fire!

This petty self is burned by conscious fire
And from the ashes, Real Self does once again aspire,
And by this bright new birth the hearts of men inspire
To so transmute this dismal dowdy world
So joy again can everywhere be heard;
All praise to thee, thou most excelling bird!

By wondrous act she does inspire my world,
It's vital I aspire to what's been heard,
Arise from sacred fire, my Phoenix bird!

Alan Jacobs

Pre-Raphaelite Poem
Pegwell Bay

The green lantern of twilight has dipped into the sea
and the grey cliffs stare full of ancient faces
among the wrinkles and crevices. Low tide.
Rocks, exposed in the shallows, recede into darkness.
On the shore, wife and second sister are intent
upon searching among the rock pools and shingle;
garrulous and homely, preservers of memories,
the perfect players of the finite role
from whom no mystery is inviolable;
wife and second sister, gatherers of seaweed,
shells and odd-coloured stones . . . dregs of a day's excursion.

By my silent sister, pale and wistful, stands apart.
Against that sea of gold-spun silk she seems
absorbed by some far away point as though
she had been waiting there for years -
the whole of our childhood is suspended there
in the dark eyes of that Penelope!

The day, nearly over, is dressed in all
its translucent finery and each of us
is engaged according to temperament
(the games are over; my son, tired, drags his spade
behind him) - and suddenly I am afraid:
what would happen if the impending darkness
claimed my silent sister, should close around her
and embrace that pale form, which even now
is merging with the gaunt cliff's shadow?

Alex Smith

My Father's Standing

My father stood for everything in sight:
the national anthem, his wife's bitchy tongue
and flying hands, his factory's mean use,
all those, in pub or at the match, less titchy
than himself; the majority he suffered.
He was game, and fair game. He had gammy eyes.

My father stood for nothing but himself.
Not Superego, not Authority,
nor that God on permanent French leave.
It's for himself my father stands for me.

And I was sore with grief to watch him die,
all tubes and bags, unrecognising sight.
He had little to give; and he took it all
on his pronounced jaw with a houndlike grin.

I have his genes and, when most needed, hope
I'll have his stomach for the last defeat.

Woll Redfern

Rondeau - the Lips of Old Ladies

The lips of old ladies are porous and runnelled
Faint lipstick lines stray down furrows etched by discontent
Filling the young with horrified aversion

Lipstick lines curve downwards like watery sickles
From fretted corners of lips that are cracked and needy
To chins that are pouched and puckered -
The lips of old ladies are ruched like old frilled collars

They say: Yes, although our mouths are cracked and needy
Intrepidly still we draw out our sticks of colour
From handbags where keys perpetually go astray
And confront our furrows and pouches:
We cannot, we cannot abjure the hope of beauty

I, too, have wedded Frivolity as St Francis did Poverty
And now I draw her to me, a barren bride
A final flowered shawl grown thin about my shoulders.

Claire Baines

Untitled

The girl sits on the loo
and reads the words
on the frosty pane
Tush
Shit
Rood
even here there's
sexual harassment

Adrian Room

White Walls of Silence

White walls of silence
stonedriven into the mind,
days to be recaptured
lest they should forever
disappear along the corridors of madness.

Cries were heard and listened to
but unintelligible they stumbled
on through the darkness of
those half moments that exist
between reality and fantasy.

And, 'Mother,' I cried
when she staggered past
on one of her journeys
in that other world.
She didn't stop or look round
and the pain carried her on
towards the edge of sadness.

The sun hangs low and red
in the evening sky
and memories of soft autumns
tumble over the words
not yet spoken.

Bernard Hebb

Banderilla

There are corridas, Kismet,
Where only women may perform,
And, when the bulls are run,
White arms drive in
The banderillas there, Kismet,
Drive them with skill and passion,
And the darts remain,
Tasselled and dangling.
I was young bull once,
And you were a picador
Who darted me.
But now I hang my head
And wait for my release.

Dean Juniper

A Green Song

We met at dinner; he renowned
Astronomer; I, a middling
Academic on tour around
The States, taking of tribal taboos
And ways of reckoning kin.

We met because his daughter and my son
Currently cohabited in sin and proposed
Marriage for breeding children.
But the astronomer and I did not discuss
Children or the future of the planet.

His renown lay in a jar of moondust
Brought by astronauts to earth
For inspection and interpretation;
But he and I did not discuss
The sun, the moon, the stars, or the planet.

That day he'd bought a vineyard;
At home I grew asparagus.
And then I talked with a biologist.
With conviction, she said the future lay
With crabs, not the testicles of men.

Crabs, she said, had invaded
Forests, rivers, hills,
And deserts, and with gills,
Lungs and carapace
Would win the planetary race.

We met at dinner, the astronomer and I,
And silently agreed that from the bonds,
Of parenthood we both were freed;
The future of the planet did lie
With us; our task was learning how to die.

Stephen Morris

Walk With My Son on Linnyshaw Moss

This moss,
where I began
is also yours.
You are the one
I must have with me here
to catch my memories
as they flow like blood
into the rough grass
from where the skylarks rise.

You can attend me
at the birth of that lost child -
can recreate the miracle of life
that dropped me in this place
and in no other.
You are the one
who shares my consciousness - ancestral memories
join us at the brain.

Those low hills call to us
across the rough
industrial landscape
where never any cowslip grew
and the tough coltsfoot
shines a braver light.

We stand together on the bank
to watch the miracle
of one Great Crested Grebe
dive for a fish
into the muddy water
of Black Leach Lodge.

Deirdre Armes Smith

My Quilted Peace

Last night as you curled up naked
perplexed you asked me:
'Anyway, what's so wrong
with a good day's work?'

And so, this morning,
sponging up the crumbs from your hasty breakfast,
I have cleared myself a space,
which while you work may provide me surface
to savour your words, their lingering bitterness.

For then, too heavy with sleep,
too happy with warmth and wine and
aftertastes of peppered cheese,
too drawn to your hips in the linen's crispness,
I did not answer, but teasingly tickled
the soft white hairs on the nape of your neck.

Then brimming my glass with a dark *amaro*
turned into rhyme your irritant question:

There was a young lass from Milan
who travelled to town in a tram:
all day in a bank
she slaved till she sank
in the arms of her lazy young man

Like idiots we laughed, bellowing like bulls
clutching our bellies as we howled and snorted,
until,
exhausted,
half-weeping, half-yawning,
we lowered the blinds on a silvery midnight,
sinking like seals
beneath the quilted peace.

Phil Davey

Rethymon

No muscular pilgrim drowning this
But a lard blue body beached on shore
Given up its breath without a wave but
Dragged with effort from the level sea.
Startled from our paperbacks, we saw
Those who ran to help, confused and
Rolling him, slapped dough into the sand
Breadcrumbing his inert flesh, each
Taking turns to suck his passive mouth
Working his arms like a broken pump.

And still the ambulance did not come
And still the clear tourist sky spoke
Of suntan oil, olives, sitting back
On balconies with chilled bottled beer.
And here was one not going home
To shake the sand out from his bags,
With all his mottled mass pressed down
Forcing an impression on the beach
Too heavy for the lightweight tides,
And next day we moved on from Rethymon.

Geraldine Harris

Quiet You Old Woman

Yellow marguerites flowers of the sun,
The sun god Helios many petalled Helios:
'He loves me, he loves me not,'
Babble the young girls,
And the children string the golden heads
Into a bouquet.
Yellow heads look to the light
But at night droop their gilded faces.
Green and yellow marguerites line the river bed,
Cover mounds of rubbish and heal the wounds of ruins.
The hens are clucking and sound like the old women
In black who come to see what I am doing.
'Kalimera, kalimera, oreos.'
The golden cock with black tail feathers
Struts out: 'Quiet you cackling hens.'
And the Greek male struts out,
'Quiet you old women.'

Valerie Conway

Fated Realisation of Time

Time is not
(as is commonly perceived)
The old dusty man, kindly old man,
with long white beard.
This I know - I have met Time.
Time came and I walked out
To meet the same.
I was beckoned from the hourglass,
motioned from the clock,
Teased from the sundial.
I recognised Time immediately.
'From where did you come?' said I.
Time cackled and would not answer.
'Now tell me, Time from where did you come?'
Time replied now, 'I have always, always been here.'
(This I knew to be a lie).
'You were invented by our ancestors.'
(I stated, sounding surer than I felt).
'I have always been here, in the sun and the moon,
in the orbit of the earth.'
Time was mocking me now.
'Reveal yourself,' I ordered. (Courage shrinking on my skin).
Time's cruel mirth cut me to the bone
I retreated to my house, head bent in defeat.
But I saw Time, thrust away.
In images of a circle, all corners and all disperses
Control ceases
Time cruelly laughs.

Caroline Robertson (14)

Sea Mist at Carbis Bay

As I can lose my fear
in the mirrors of other people's eyes.
I can lose myself in this sea mist,

wide open to fate
like a stone, or water,
a piece of paper stone might fold into a boat shape,

bobbing about in that space
where the sea and sky press against one another,
like love and a bone.

Sea mist puts its hand over me
like a chloroformed handkerchief,
the sky on its side in a puddle of sleep.

The time to stand
with my hands by my sides and say,
'I have it all to begin again.'

Kay Fletcher

Night Lands

The jackboot of the dusk kicks
the feeble day into
a future time
as the land crosses
the frontier of the night
into a new dimension . . .
into the night lands.

Under a black arc
etched with the acid
points of stars
the countryside sleeps
as in damp fields
cattle stir uneasily
while the hungry owl
swoops on his night-time meal.

In the city, far away,
the homeless settle for their rest
huddling on hard pavement beds
in cardboard boxes, wrapped
in their tattered rags
and day old copies of the Sun . . .
they sink into their sad
forsaken sleep
under the blanket
of the stars.

Stephen Gyles

Pips

Shaped to want,
matching the cupped hand
coolly, the apple's lightened
of its rind

by the knife;
the quick blade unpacks
the centre from a green
and gauzy helix

till the sodden pulp
is all that's left,
bar an incongruous stalk
and leafy tuft.

Victory scented, the tongue
weeps impatience
till its stooped
and pouted mouth claims

its prey. Furrow-like
it turns the flesh,
but brings no new seed
to heal the gash

it leaves; and at the core,
the damage done, spits
back out the podded sachet's
useless pips.

David Wheatley

Loving Pains

I'd like to take the pain without complaint,
And willingly to suffer, like I should,
In drama or tragedy. I want to be good
Playing the fool, the sinner or the saint.
And you could watch and tease with your restraint,
Or tantalise and torture if you would.
Your purity and cruelty mixed, if it could
Be ever, in grey and black, - dark and faint.
And if you ever ask where I find the joy
In such a love, I'll answer you for sure:
There's nothing like the pleasure of the boy
Who's left alone, forsaken, hurt and poor;
Because in every new trick you employ,
There's the ecstasy of torment like before.

Richard Chapman

The Edible Seaside

Everywhere you look there is food,
Shop windows are gold with pastries
or gleaming hoards of foil wrapped sweets.
In the spangled confectionery shops
Magpie-eyes pluck out Sugar ships;
small clammy hands open out
into precious flowers of soft chocolate.
Consumption is a desperate, barbaric attack.
People impale chips on wooden prongs
like Eskimos hunting for fish.
Mouths tear at crystallised doughnuts
and munch and crunch and chew.
The gutters are cluttered with polystyrene coffins
splattered with tomato sauce
and the remains of ravished burgers.
On the beach they dig their toes
into the moist fudge of sand
and pink sausage fingers
pat the ground into castles and pies.
Children tease candyfloss with their tongues
baring their teeth like vicious dogs.

Gaia Holmes

I Smoke

The crumpled ash of candlelit
hysteria, stemmed
violence hallows the balcony.

Raging sailors playing out
a manicured fight
on the chequered board

shriek to one another,
a crossfire
moving to perfection.

I am fine, actor and victim
at perception time.
Like a hairpin split in two.

Interference, air waves
whose blurred edges
block the inside of my eyes.

I am pummelled out by noise
in frantic action,
the world departs, loses poise.

The shining kitchen hatch
shadows solitary
figures, masking guests.

Matriarchs stir the cauldron,
gossip and guard
loose bones of past visions.

Do you remember the sand and
the sea? Daddy laughing, Mummy
tucking away the tears . . .

Open another window, enter the dark.

Patrick Williamson

Untitled

It was those years, we were listening to music
of a past decade on our wide balconies
agonising we might follow the
destiny of the spirit of the beehive . . .
the life of the ants was murmuring in our ears
transforming into sorrow our picture - we were scared.
The spirit of the boy returned to the small church
                                        of the past century
there where he played with the children making
                                        huts out of canes
in his hair some grass was forgotten
and some twigs from blackberry bushes
his face was stained by berries
The plants inside their pots observed our balcony
The pebbles at the seashore fell from the hand
                                        one after the other
On the seats, the women were studying their maps
 - a possible journey, to Rome perhaps, possibly theatre
Tomorrow we will not be here any more
The plants nodded positively and
the girl sitting next to the urn
moved the end of her foot that was
caught in the sandal

E G Brewster

Göreme

The spirit moved on the face of the rock,
The dense mineral ocean, questing faults,
For its purpose. Burrowed it, riddled it,
Termite towers and parched siracs.
This was a landscape for the lives of saints
Celled and serrated, at home
In Cappadocia. The rooted vine and fig
Can hardly hold the earth,
But the intenser air tingles
With the high voltages of prayer.

N K Sandars

Taking Photos at the Taxidermist

The glare off the back of the stuffed, silver bass
Pulled me in. 'Can I help ya?' he said in a slow, Texas accent.
'No thanks, just lookin,' I answered.
'Can I take a few photos,' I asked.
'Sure, sure go ahead,' came his formaldehyde reply.

Sound of camera, then roar, of . . . what? I glanced a flick of
tongue and
Near my foot saw the only animal alive in the taxidermist shop.
A caged, about five foot long, Texas diamond-backed
rattlesnake or an old 'Rattler'.
He amongst the dead shadow shells of animals, with his
fifteen rattles,
Thundering his indignation, a dots and dashes code to vacant
listeners.

Asking a resurrection, the spitting out of Taxidermist' Death stuffings.
I took my photos (probably blurred) slightly shaken and left
thinking I'd seen
A black winged bird flying and marbled-grey fish jumping
darkly in the corner.
Waiting closing time, when the old coyote laughing and rolling
in the distant
Desert sand, howled, having heard the padlock drift to the
wooden floor.

Over the edge, his belly tickled cool across the cages door, the
snake found his way,
Coiling silently behind the tall, hand tooled, brown cowboy boots.
Around half-time,
As the man lost in the Saturday afternoon game, sipping a beer,
followed the football
Through the air and reached for his boots; fast fangs fastened.
His surprised eyes rolled and glassed.
His beer can spilled, wobbling in the wind of the slow turning
ceiling fan.

They found him the next day on the porch; one boot on, the
other inside.
The sheriff turned the TV off. An autopsy discovered two small,
deep holes between his legs.
I developed my film. A blank roll. And somewhere in a small
Texas town a snake still crawls coolly,
And sunset tales are told by Mexicans of lights in the desert
And sometimes on the cliff's smiling painted face can be read
Wilderness - 1; Man - 0 . . .
. . . Next game?

Buster Tripp

The Final Embrace

as you stand there, thinner now
I remember nine years passing
see each minute edging over

you look taller now, gaunt
bleached and bruised
sick or sickening

for the first time
I can see
the bones beneath your skin

the places where
you once
had flesh

I recall those late night conversations
- sarcasm and smiles -
seek in desperation

a single laughter line
but cannot smile
even touch you

fear
the years
to come:

the final embrace.

K P McIntyre

Bromeliad

In the fever of the forest
Where fiery sun attempts in vain
To pierce the canopy of leaves,
Spreading in patchwork -
Shades of green,
High above the fibrous floor,
They bloom flamboyantly,
Whilst thirstily awaiting rain.
Jungle flowers of brilliance,
Intense, amazing epiphytes
With equally exotic names,
Earth star, Queen's Tears, and Flaming Sword,
Who live in harmony with trees,
Adorn the latticework of boughs
With colourful displays
That vie with grandiose attire
Of shrieking parakeets.
Succulent leaves of many shades,
Banded with purple, silver, white,
Or shimmering red beneath each straplike frond.
There, nestling in each patterned cup
A flower, like some festive candle glows
Shining, showy, sensational
Flaunting its beauty today
For tomorrow, forever, it fades.

Derry Veal

Sonnet (After Milton) on a True Happening

'Better be alive and blind than dead.'
Thus the surgeon spoke: his fateful choice
removed the eyes of Nicholas. A voice
in painful love, his mother's, proudly said:
'My child will be a blind boy who can see.'
The small boy Nicholas then bravely sighed
aloud, 'I loved to watch the moon and sea,
Now I may fall in!' Her voice replied:
'You'll never walk alone, but are always free
to choose.' His fragile spirit soared. He cried
out, heard; he felt, he touched, in darkness knew
the power of family love would always guide
him; precious life among the chosen few.
His mother's hope: a blind boy who will see.

Louise J Rosenberg

Two Rivers

The River Stour glides through broad fields of wheat
Where harvest workers saw his boat and raised
Their hats to Hardy in those bygone days.

Today pleasure craft around Manhattan
Steer clear of bridges that they cannot pass
Without provoking rocks and bottles
Rained down upon them by the underclass.

John Mallows

To Where the Wheat

Shredded wheat moved to their country
Their daily bread of fields afar
Breaking bread together
Get us off our knees
Knees bent upwards
While Body resting in meadows
Shredded memories of movies unassembled
Praying mountains peaks of granite waves
Our daily bread on the move
Cargo this year, next,
While pasture flowers
Grace it grows.

Rita Ann Unger

Birthmark

Blotched, red, ink.
The life is spread on a single page,
Yet it consumes the entire notepad
A multifaced accident.

The birthmark,
What an indelible stamp,
No clear patterning
Yet, regal, it sees itself.

Holding the sceptre firmly
Its head sweeps over the remaining words,
They feel like puppets in their own old territory.
Individualess - just a mass of symbolic scribbles.

Although, red is the colour mark,
Purple esteems forth.
The crown breathes heavily to the call of this duty.
This blotch has taken hold of life.

I've tried avoidance
The page opens the same.
Tear it, scrub it, burn it, throw it out.
The damage has eroded the pages.

This birthmark is here to stay
Its parents have been chosen
Like the selection of a jury
Number, random, selected by accident.

That's the way the birthmark likes it.

Amanda Creque

Lullaby?

An almost full and terracotta moon
hangs low and heavy
a pregnancy detached and floating
free of mother
floods me as a sense of permanence

To have been there always
The penny weighting quiet unnumbered tongues
The gasp shape opening each life.

No sense now of the wan communion wafer white
that spangles through stories and pictures,
the milk bottle top on the nativity collage.
This is solid, terra firma,
and this particular light will never happen again.

Sarcophagus ochre sets off the great sad face
A mask of surprise or shock
suspicions about the party well before
the light came on.
Tonight's precarious tilt deepens any emotion
I want it to feel
An angle of madness, Ophelia drooling.
The angle of the analyst registering understanding.

Moon words are metal
'silver', 'golden', 'shining', 'cool'.
Tonight rust makes it precious,
recoverable, an investment,
the heirloom patient in attic darkness.

Lying back I re-run its image, its effect
the beauty like the certainty I can't enough express
the unrepeatable joke, 'You had to be there.'

Pat Cunningham

Trees

(a meditation in September)

In autumn trees put out flags.

They are lovely, as Mary was lovely,
beautiful as, in their flowering time,
Cleopatra and Helen were beautiful.
Serene, as Gotoma was serene.

Their elegance mocks us as we walk in their shade.

They are old as rock is old.
Their branches span the centuries,
their roots anchor us to earth,
they breathe and we breathe too.

They are our gentle ancestors,

colonised a world wider
than any imagined by Alexander,
by Rome's imperial legions,
or the Great Khan's tireless horsemen.

They obey naturally the Five Precepts,

take nothing which is not freely given,
but shelter the weak, feed the hungry,
returning good for evil
offer no violence to the violent.

Their silence rebukes our cacophony.

In green twilight of great forests
we walk in awe,
our voices lost among their rafters.
Death, which harries us, brushes them lightly.

John Ward

Social Disease

Old boys known as young men
'Hang round' that hot-dog stand
Swap viruses then
Dream of stolen car radios wanted
Which they cough up for in anyone's hand
And despite the threat remain undaunted.

But everyday one dies away
To be replaced by a new face
Who will wait to Saturday to stray
Unless responsibility can claim the unpure
And their image cardiacs without a trace.

Rest still parental doctors
Nearly four hundred men are
Squabbling over the cure.

Matthew Brolly

Nowhere to be

Once she felt the warmth
of her blood held herself straight
skin smooth firm-set people said
she had honey on her tongue

now shivers run
down her spine she can't stop
screeching like an alley cat
on her knees in the dust slashed

and scratched by devils
clutching in her hand a piece
of coarse dry grass uprooted
flattened nowhere to be refugee.

Joan Maizels

Our First Walk

(On discovering a brother, unknown for fifty years)

Just as the fawns leap into space
So you my brother burst into my world.
They chase, race across the meadow
as your words move around my heart.
Excited, free, they rush up hill and down,
My spirits rise in tune with them,
as quickly sink in disbelief.
    But they capture all we've lost,
    the expectation of a full-fledged life.
    We look backwards, try to salvage
    from those hidden years, our common father.
    Memories haunt, elude, lie buried,
    will not surface as fully as you'd wish.
Elegant gracious creatures
you move exquisitely through this green field
bringing new life in the mists of spring.

Rosemary Hoggett

Finglas

Pea pods, stone slabs, wires of old cane
and in the sunlight the shimmer of a green leaf,
a climbing beanstalk, hovering above old heads.
My reach could gather no success
in the granny's council Eden
so I waited eagerly for tit-bits
from the garden-hanging fruits above me.
I tasted, gingerly at first, the sweet
Sugar Snap and the infant broad bean
and in the ground, rooting for light,
were the deep red beets I was told
would turn my unsunned pallor
to the colour of a bright lipstick.
I wondered at the creeping vines
grandfather twisted from his window
and sucked plums over plans for his escape.
There was loose talk he would never walk again
and like the vine crawling to his attentions
the years would grow and caress him.
I laughed when they buried him in the ground.

George Wakefield

Pretty Little Thing

She was a pretty little thing
Some said a genius
Who could talk to many nations
But I didn't trust her
For come upon her quietly
And you could hear her whisper
'. . . come quick . . . come quick . . . come quick . . .'

She was a pretty little thing
Some said a mystic
Who could talk to long dead people
But I didn't trust her
For come upon her quietly
And you could hear her whisper
' . . . this world . . . this world . . . this world . . .'

She was a pretty little thing
Some said a healer
Who could touch a person healthy
But I didn't trust her
For come upon her quietly
And you could hear her whisper
' . . . kill them . . . kill them . . . kill them . . . '

Peter Barns

Madness, Longing and Desire

In the movie theatre, the couple sits,
arms resting not upon the same rest,
an uncomfortable fit.
Silent, they watch the film,
and as it ends, they are slow to home.

The plane that crashes and burns,
and miles away, a breath carries
the slight debris of ash
dusting the drying summer's grass.

The nightly news, the souring milk,
the refrigerator with its open door,
the shoes kicked off on the living room floor.
Passionless, and to dismiss,
it is not hard to use a kiss
as a cattle prod.

To steel yourself, to age alone,
and home is just a place to sleep.
In sleep comes the sound,
the hollow sound
of easy weeping, the voice your own.
And in the end.
the agonal breaths that rest and throw,
keeping time to the final question:
    What was it?
    Now, now you know.

It was madness.
It was longing.
It was desire.

Maryanne R Kichuk

M E

A misshapen consciousness
        opaque and grotesque
As a distorted reflection
        in a polluted pool;
A confusion of meaning
        in a nerve poisoned being,
Short circuiting wire
        in a metabolic mire,
A pale, sickly mindlight
        like a flickering striplight,
A hissing cassette
        of repetitive groans.

Del Kennedy

Art Forms

When I was Gauguin and more
The pictures fell off my fingers
And did not form as art must form
From all that has gone before
But from nothing such that nothing formed
As if abstract but not abstracted from
The elements of light that frame
Each atom of your look beneath
The glass: I take it then that pictures
Rise in value with your words
Which hang in all our galleries
Suspended, unattached and at a loss
To prise the paint from where the painter
As creator limned the unknown light
And as a God of layers made it seen.

Sean O'Connor

Chasing Dragons

Dragon's breath touched my face
when he dared me chase him
and led away down neon streets
saw sparrows fall exhausted
as tables turned and dragon's
smoke became a dragon's curse.

Sheree Sartain

Ovid

When you undress
I am like Ovid in the bed.
Magician of changes, charmed
by your own transformation.
The shapes you put on
with your clothes
on the floor.

Do not assume
that when my eyes are closed
I do not see you.
Do not assume I cannot hear.
I know your touch,
the kiss of flesh
at the tip of your breast.

The chill of your hand,
the shapes you adopt
at the moments of silence,
when the curtains part
at the touch of the wind.
You ache to slip away tonight
but I will hold you
to whatever form you take.

Until, like a darkened city
you are completed.
Whole in a new element,
transformed by it.
Moving as a fish does
in deep water.
Oblivious to my fear of drowning.

David Stenhouse

Poet

After writing some poems and publishing
a couple of them, he decided
that poetry was too much hard work. And too boring,
poring for hours over words.

So he decided to concentrate his creative energies on
being poetic. He read *Lives of Poets.*
He got good at mooning around
like a lovesick boy, fasting,
wandering at night, drinking himself to ruin,
blasting *Bolero* and *Don Giovanni* fifty-three times over.
Of course, he dressed down for the part.

He fell in love with himself and
everybody else fell in love with him too.

Lots of people want to sleep with a poet, he found,
and as this was all he was in it for anyway,
he was happy.

He was the greatest writer he'd ever met.
That good.

Brian Daldorph

The Old Father

The whispered reminiscence breezes softly through the room
like gossamer strands on gentle currents.
Ageless faces of an age gone by
transporting the present to wrap it in time.

Soporific seconds glide silently over
the face of the peaceful old man,
stroking the staccato moment as a host
of generations peer down on their protected history.

All gnarled and rotten the frame now
once beautiful and free,
with rusting spring and autumn's fading light
the grand father stutters . . .
then stops in dead of night.

The timeless tunnel now reveals
a blissful shining star,
and the eager faces greet their guest
and carry him afar to leave the
whispered reminiscence
long, long into future lives
of the lonely ones now left behind.

Andrew Paton

The Other Side of Europe

'We've heard it all before,' we say
And let the news from Bosnia pass by like some irrelevancy.
Compassion fatigue is the state of play -
The scenes familiar, constant press intrusion an indecency.

The other side of Europe is not so far away.
'They look like us,' we say and so they do.
But eyes are dark, the faces gaunt and grey,
That wistful look, pleading, uncomprehending too.

That haunted look that will not go away,
That haunted look that goes with battered suitcase -
Transportable belongings, essential things for every day,
Scrambled together and more precious still when homes are gone.

There is no outside enemy, the bitter foe is one
Who was once neighbour, colleague, trusted friend.
His hallmark cruelty without restraint, unbridled -
Calculating and unfeeling in a war that knows no end.

Ghost towns and villages bear witness to the fear
Of thousands who have joined the rank of refugee.
Toys scattered, washing on a line -
Reminders of the haste with which a family had to flee.

Ceasefires - such flimsy things soon broken
And then the product of great minds, deep thought -
Yet unacceptable and like a dream Utopian -
Vance-Owen Peace Plan - Dashed hopes. War continues
to be fought.

The other side of Europe is not so far away.
'Why, they're like us,' we say and so they are!
Their fate unknown, homeland in disarray,
Hopes dashed forever in the bitterness of war.

Eleanor Trotter

To Half a Rubber Ball - Mistakenly Taken for a Tortoise

In the wild grass she lay, as I
was looking for my cat; the eye
caught her suddenly, unexpected
And still, a dark-hued reality,
a blot of ink in the surrounding
greenness.
I was about to call my cat,
educate her;
acquaint her feline character with the
creeping
creatures, stuck to Mother Earth - but she
wouldn't listen, heeded
my call too late. I had drawn closer
already; the eye had lied.
What distance made a sleeping tortoise
proved just a Rubber Ball;
black, motionless, buried
to the waist; a sordid sight, unfit
for a young Cat; I recoiled.

Dionysios Divaris

An Ordinary Day

An ordinary day shopping, in a local street
Rounding a corner suddenly faced
With a dark red pool, sticky,
Expanding from the gutter. In it
White, torn tissues, used to stem the flow
Twitch in the breeze. Fragile and futile as moth's wings.
Swarms of police cars, uniformed men, hovering
Like blue bees around red honey
Aftermath of an inexplicable act.

It was all over.
But the shockwaves could still be felt.
One shopkeeper, tight-lipped said little,
Reluctant, afraid, or just plain shocked.
His brother, the newsagent next-door said, shaken,
'I thought it was a joke at first,'
Repeating, unable to absorb this news firsthand,
Before his papers sensationalise,
Embellish beyond recognition
Parcelling this act for human consumption.
'I thought it was a joke at first.
When the machetes appeared.'

In such a way violence erupts into our lives
Reminder that the snapshots accompanying headlines
Of missing, injured, shot or mugged
Were taken by someone's wife, mother, husband, lover
Against the blurred background, for them all too familiar
That means home: their life,
Now irreparably changed.

Cathy Spiers

Lullaby

Your orange-peel buttocks on my thighs,
My nose between your shoulders - spooned in sleep.

And my old knob hangs groundward, sheathed in death,
Like some driver ankle-trapped in wreckage.

Constantly, other faces, other mouths
Offer the one thing you can't: change from you.

As if upon the ridge of some isthmus,
Not knowing what I want, but wanting what I've known.

Peter J Smith

A Hanging

Woken by the daylight's traffic
In a steel and azure sky,
She sickens and spurns
Her twenty-third hour gone by.
        Heat begins, the quick
Trade of rope and ladder
        Nears; her mind burns.

She fingers her prison, looks out
To the lemon-bread parade grounds
Where death's one O hangs
On a question mark. The sounds
        Of marching, a shout
To stop before her number;
        Keys trap her hands.

And then she paces into the light,
Blinded by remembrance,
Told to climb and stand
Thoughtless before the breezy dance
        Of dumb rope. So tight
Around her neck, the noose -
        Then that dark man.

Scott Anderson

Eden Saw Made

My soul says that I do not consent
To live in Paradise but prefer to Fall
In pain through the infinite abyss
Outside the Gates.

And that is why I do not like the silence,
So says my soul,
Because in the silence I hear His voice
Calling in the garden my Holy Name.
The scream in the abyss,
- which Munch and later Bacon heard -
Affords diversion.

And this is why I am afraid of darkness.
In the darkness I can see my nakedness
(There is nothing to distract my eyes)
And I am ashamed.
Better then to live by neon lights
And be illumined

In a sense.

Michael Carrick Dunne

Prayer to Jasmine

In sleepless nights, I felt inside me, drop
        by drop, my innocence take shape.
So one day in my antique youth, I went
        to search for what the world forgot.
In a distant sun-scorched land, Paradise was there
in the jasmine that sprang forth from a tree in Hell.
I had found my amulet, found my sword and shield.

Then with my new and vibrant youth, I called
        my bitter, second self, my soul.
A woman, blooming with a golden liquid health,
        appeared among the sand and foam.
Later, farther from the sea, with a swoon I fell
trembling and I kissed her warm, silver lunar skin.
Morning brought me what, 'til then, I had not deserved.

Alone now, weightless, down along the shore,
        I called the promise of her name.
An eagle overhead cried out to me:
        'Not yet! Your heart must be like mine.'
Cloisterless, I began the sad and holy task,
to avenge each wasted spring and each gentle breeze
not allowed to become a gesture or a deed.

To you, who in the darkness were a flame
        descending one Sunday to me,
I pray that I be worthy of your smell,
        that I be faithful to your light.
Give me strength now while the sun hides behind the clouds,
while I wander in the north, singing bitter songs,
and around me, people dream of a distant heart.

Thomas Sarantos